My First NFL Book

MINNESOTA VIKINGS

Steven M. Karras

www.av2books.com

LET'S READ

AV²
BY WEIGL™

ADDED VALUE • AUDIO VISUAL

Go to **www.av2books.com**, and enter this book's unique code.

BOOK CODE

H726287

AV² by Weigl brings you media enhanced books that support active learning.

AV² provides enriched content that supplements and complements this book. Weigl's AV² books strive to create inspired learning and engage young minds in a total learning experience.

Your AV² Media Enhanced books come alive with...

Audio
Listen to sections of the book read aloud.

Video
Watch informative video clips.

Embedded Weblinks
Gain additional information for research.

Try This!
Complete activities and hands-on experiments.

Key Words
Study vocabulary, and complete a matching word activity.

Quizzes
Test your knowledge.

Slide Show
View images and captions, and prepare a presentation.

... and much, much more!

Published by AV² by Weigl
350 5th Avenue, 59th Floor
New York, NY 10118

Website: www.av2books.com

Library of Congress Control Number: 2017930694

ISBN 978-1-4896-5523-3 (hardcover)
ISBN 978-1-4896-5525-7 (multi-user eBook)

Printed in the United States of America in Brainerd, Minnesota
1 2 3 4 5 6 7 8 9 0 21 20 19 18 17

032017
020317

Editor: Katie Gillespie
Art Director: Terry Paulhus

Weigl acknowledges Getty Images and iStock as the primary image suppliers for this title.

My First NFL Book

MINNESOTA VIKINGS

CONTENTS

2 AV² Book Code
4 Team History
6 The Stadium
8 Team Spirit
10 The Jerseys
12 The Helmet
14 The Coach
16 Player Positions
18 Star Player
19 Famous Player
20 Team Records
22 By the Numbers
24 Quiz/Log on to
    www.av2books.com

Team History

The Minnesota Vikings started playing in the NFL in 1960. Their first head coach was Norm Van Brocklin. He was an NFL quarterback before he became a coach. The Vikings won their first championship in 1970 under coach Bud Grant.

The Vikings' defense was nicknamed the "Purple People Eaters" in the 1960s.

usbank
stadium
usbank
stadium
SHORTER WAIT TIME
ADDITIONAL
LINES
4
5
6
7
SMITH
22
ALLEN
69
ALLEN
69
29
CLEAN BAGS ONLY

The Stadium

The Vikings' home field is U.S. Bank Stadium. It was built in 2016. The stadium has a roof to keep out the cold. There are 66,200 seats. U.S. Bank Stadium will host the 52nd Super Bowl in 2018.

U.S. Bank Stadium in Minneapolis, Minnesota, is the team's third stadium.

Team Spirit

Viktor the Viking is the team's mascot. He likes to give high fives to Vikings fans. Viktor can often be seen waving the team's flag on the field before home games. He has been the Vikings' mascot since 2007.

Viktor carries a wooden pole with a football attached.

The Jerseys

The Vikings' colors are purple, gold, and white. Home jerseys are purple with white numbers. Away jerseys are white with purple numbers. The top stripe on the sleeve is wider at the end to look like a Viking horn. The Vikings started wearing these jerseys in 2013.

The Helmet

The Vikings' helmets are matte purple. Matte means that the color is not shiny. A white Viking horn logo is on both sides of the helmet. There are speakers in the quarterback's helmet so he can get plays from the coach.

The Vikings' helmets got a new design in 2006 to make the logo stand out more.

13

The Coach

Mike Zimmer has been the Vikings' head coach since 2014. This is his first time being an NFL head coach. Zimmer was the offensive coordinator for three other NFL teams before joining the Vikings. Zimmer is the Vikings' ninth head coach.

Player Positions

Each NFL team has 11 players on the field at one time. Every play starts when the center gives the ball to the quarterback. This is called a snap. The special teams come onto the field when a team is going to kick the ball.

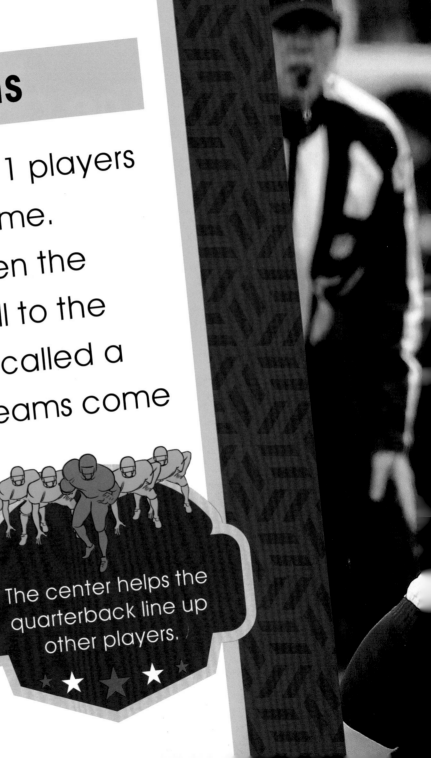

The center helps the quarterback line up other players.

Stefon Diggs is a wide receiver. His role is to catch passes from the quarterback. Diggs played his first game with the Vikings in 2015. He set an NFL record by catching passes for at least 85 yards in each of his first four games. Diggs also set a team record in 2016 for the most catches in a November game.

Fran Tarkenton played quarterback for the Vikings in the 1960s and 1970s. He threw four touchdown passes and scored a touchdown in his first game. Tarkenton was with the team for 14 seasons. He led the Vikings to three Super Bowls. Tarkenton was added to the Pro Football Hall of Fame in 1986.

Famous Player

Team Records

The Vikings have played in four Super Bowls. Fred Cox is the Vikings' all-time leading scorer. He was a kicker who scored 1,365 points in his career. Cris Carter is another famous Viking who played wide receiver. No other Viking has matched his career record of 110 touchdowns.

4 Super Bowls

Fred Cox

1,365 Points

Cris Carter

110 Touchdowns

By the Numbers

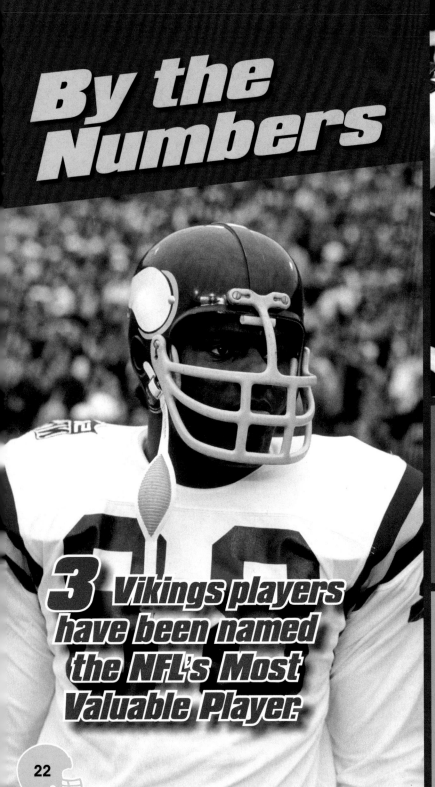

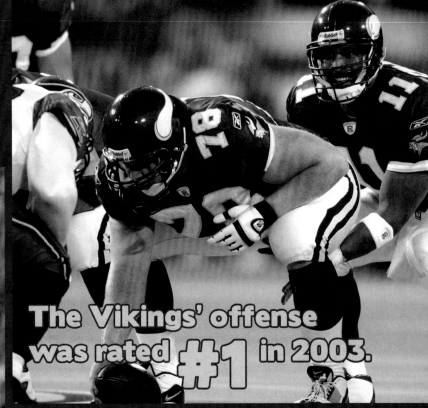

The Vikings' offense was rated **#1** in 2003.

The Vikings' **biggest** win was in 1963 when they beat the Cleveland Browns **51-3**.

3 Vikings players have been named the NFL's Most Valuable Player.

The largest crowd at a Vikings home game was **64,482** people in 2003.

U.S. Bank Stadium has a Viking ship that is **159 feet** tall.

13

Vikings are in the Pro Football Hall of Fame.

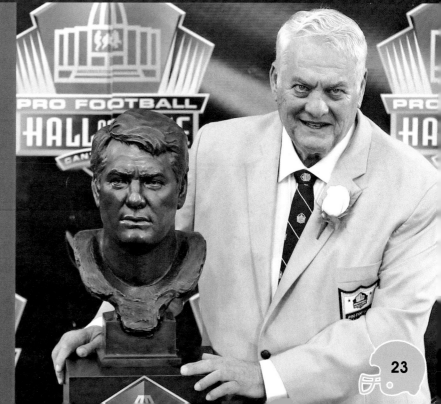

Quiz

1. What was the Vikings' defense nicknamed in the 1960s?

2. In what city is U.S. Bank Stadium?

3. What is attached to Viktor the Viking's wooden pole?

4. How many touchdown passes did Fran Tarkenton throw in his first Vikings game?

5. How many points did Fred Cox score during his career with the Vikings?

ANSWERS 1. The Purple People Eaters 2. Minneapolis 3. A football 4. Four 5. 1,365